Boing! Boing! Where could you watch
kangaroos jumping?

The **continent** of Australia!
A continent is a big piece of land.

Arctic Ocean

North America

Atlantic Ocean

Pacific Ocean

South America

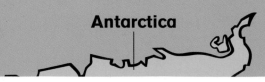

Antarctica

4

PULL AHEAD BOOKS
Continents

AUSTRALIA

by Madeline Donaldson

2 t
- 3

- 5

Lerner

L   Books • London • New York • Minneapolis

This book was first published in the United States of America in 2005.
First published in the United Kingdom in 2008 by
Lerner Books,
Dalton House,
60 Windsor Avenue,
London SW19 2RR

Website address: www.lernerbooks.co.uk

This edition was updated and edited for UK publication by Discovery Books Ltd., Unit 3, 37 Watling Street, Leintwardine, Shropshire SY7 0LW

Words in **bold type** are explained in a glossary on page 30.

British Library Cataloguing in Publication Data

Donaldson, Madeline
  Australia. - (Pull ahead books. Continents)
  1. Australia - Juvenile literature 2. Australia - Pictorial
works - Juvenile literature
  I. Title
  994

  ISBN-13: 978 1 58013 333 3

Photographs are used with the permission of: © Otto Rogge/CORBIS, p. 3; © Paul Souders/ WorldFoto, pp. 6, 7, 9, 15, 16–17, 20, 22; © Bill Bachman, pp. 8, 10, 13, 14, 21; © David Fleetham/Visuals Unlimited, p. 11; © Jean-Paul Ferrero/AUSCAPE, p. 12; © Theo Allofs/ Visuals Unlimited, p. 18; © D. Parer & E. Parer-Cook/AUSCAPE, p. 19; © John Kreul/ Independent Picture Service, pp. 23, 24, 26–27; © Michael Jensen/AUSCAPE, p. 25. Maps on pp. 4–5 and 29 by Laura Westlund.

Printed in China

There are seven continents on Earth.
Australia is the smallest.

Australia is the only continent that is also a **country**. Australia's **capital** city is Canberra.

The island of Tasmania is also part of Australia. This is a forest of eucalyptus trees on Tasmania.

Oceans surround Australia on all sides.

Surf's up! Australians swim and surf in the continent's oceans.

Off the north-eastern coast of Australia is the Great Barrier Reef. It is the world's largest **coral reef**.

Animals called corals live in the warm waters around the reef.

The highest parts of Australia are in the south and east.

Catch air! Australians enjoy skiing and snowboarding there in the winter.

Farmers grow wheat in the lowest parts of Australia. This land lies near the middle of the continent.

Deserts cover much of western
Australia. Watch out for snakes like
the desert death adder!

The grasslands of western Australia
feed huge herds of cattle and sheep.
These are merino sheep.

They are kicking
up dust as they go
into a paddock, or
holding area.

Remember the jumping kangaroos?

They are **marsupials.** Marsupials raise their babies in pouches.

18

Platypuses are found only in
Australia. They have a wide,
flat nose called a snout.

Munch! Munch!
This koala is
eating the
leaves of a
eucalyptus tree.

Acacia trees are found all over
Australia. Some kinds of acacia trees
have bright flowers.

Most Australians live in large cities along the coasts. Sydney is the continent's biggest city.

One of Sydney's famous buildings is the **opera** house. Here, singers perform in musical plays called operas.

Few people live in the **outback**. This is the open countryside in the middle of Australia.

Zoom! Some people in the outback
get around by aeroplane.

Australia has many interesting parts! Do you know about Ayers Rock? The **Aborigines**, or first Australians, call the huge rock Uluru.

There's always something new to learn about Australia!

Facts about Australia

- Australia covers almost 8 million square kilometres (3 million square miles).

- The animals of Australia include echidnas, kangaroos, koalas, kookaburras, platypuses, Tasmanian devils and wallabies.

- Plants living in Australia include acacia (or wattle) trees, eucalyptus (or gum) trees and grass trees.

- About 20 million people live in Australia. Nearly all of them speak English.

- Aborigines make up a very small part—only 1 per cent—of Australia's 20 million people.

- The large cities of Australia are Sydney, Brisbane, Melbourne, Perth and Adelaide. Canberra is the capital city.

Map of Australia

Indian Ocean

Pacific Ocean

Great Barrier Reef

Great Sandy Desert

Outback

Central Lowlands

Brisbane

Great Victoria Desert

Perth

Adelaide

Sydney

Canberra

Melbourne

Indian Ocean

Tasmania

Glossary

Aborigines: a group of people who were the first to live in Australia

capital: a city where a government is based

continent: one of seven big pieces of land on Earth

coral reef: an area of coral rocks that lies near the surface of the ocean. Coral rocks are the skeletons of once living animals called corals.

country: a place where people live and share the same laws

marsupials: animals whose females carry their babies in a pouch on the mother's stomach

opera: a play set to music and sung by singers

outback: the open countryside of central Australia

Further Reading and Website

Bell, Rachel. *Australia* (Visit to...) Heinemann, 2003.

Davis, Kevin A. *Look What Came from Australia* (Look What Came From) Franklin Watts, 2000.

Fox, Mary Virginia. *Australia* (Continents) Heinemann, 2006.

Fox, Mary. *Australia and Oceania* (Heinemann First Library: Continents) Heinemann Library, 2007

Parker, Vicky. *Australia* (We're From) Heinemann Library, 2006.

Pyres, Greg. *Coral Reef Explorer* (Habitat Explorer) Raintree, 2004.

Richardson, Margot. *Australia* (Letters from Around the World) Cherrytree Books, 2004.

Royston, Angela. *Deserts* (My World of Geography) Heinemann Library, 2005.

Spilsbury, Louise A. and Richard Spilsbury *Watching Kangaroos in Australia* (Wild World), Heinemann, 2006.

Theodorou, Rod. *Koalas* (Animals in Danger) Heinemann Library, 2001.

Enchanted Learning

http://enchantedlearning.com/geography/australia
The geography section of this website has links to every continent.

Index